NATIONAL GEOGRAPHIC

Push or Pull?

John Parker

Why does the sailboat move?

The wind **pushes** the sailboat.

Why does the sled move?

The dogs **pull** the sled.

The water **pushes** the waterwheel.

Why does the train move?

The engine **pulls** the train.

9

Why do the rocks move?

The front-end loader **pushes** the rocks.

Why does the trailer move?

The truck pulls the trailer.

13

Why does the ship move?

The tugboat **pushes** the ship.

15

Pull